HowE

Mini Hummingbird Gardening Guide

7 Steps to Hummingbird Gardening

HowExpert with Essie Thorn

**Copyright HowExpert™
www.HowExpert.com**

For more tips related to this topic, visit HowExpert.com/hummingbird.

Recommended Resources

- HowExpert.com – Quick 'How To' Guides on All Topics from A to Z by Everyday Experts.
- HowExpert.com/free – Free HowExpert Email Newsletter.
- HowExpert.com/books – HowExpert Books
- HowExpert.com/courses – HowExpert Courses
- HowExpert.com/membership – HowExpert Membership Site
- HowExpert.com/writers – Write About Your #1 Passion/Knowledge/Expertise & Become a HowExpert Author.
- HowExpert.com/resources – Additional HowExpert Recommended Resources
- YouTube.com/HowExpert – Subscribe to HowExpert YouTube.
- Instagram.com/HowExpert – Follow HowExpert on Instagram.
- Facebook.com/HowExpert – Follow HowExpert on Facebook.

COPYRIGHT, LEGAL NOTICE AND DISCLAIMER:

COPYRIGHT © BY HOWEXPERT™ (OWNED BY HOT METHODS). ALL RIGHTS RESERVED WORLDWIDE. NO PART OF THIS PUBLICATION MAY BE REPRODUCED IN ANY FORM OR BY ANY MEANS, INCLUDING SCANNING, PHOTOCOPYING, OR OTHERWISE WITHOUT PRIOR WRITTEN PERMISSION OF THE COPYRIGHT HOLDER.

DISCLAIMER AND TERMS OF USE: PLEASE NOTE THAT MUCH OF THIS PUBLICATION IS BASED ON PERSONAL EXPERIENCE AND ANECDOTAL EVIDENCE. ALTHOUGH THE AUTHOR AND PUBLISHER HAVE MADE EVERY REASONABLE ATTEMPT TO ACHIEVE COMPLETE ACCURACY OF THE CONTENT IN THIS GUIDE, THEY ASSUME NO RESPONSIBILITY FOR ERRORS OR OMISSIONS. ALSO, YOU SHOULD USE THIS INFORMATION AS YOU SEE FIT, AND AT YOUR OWN RISK. YOUR PARTICULAR SITUATION MAY NOT BE EXACTLY SUITED TO THE EXAMPLES ILLUSTRATED HERE; IN FACT, IT'S LIKELY THAT THEY WON'T BE THE SAME, AND YOU SHOULD ADJUST YOUR USE OF THE INFORMATION AND RECOMMENDATIONS ACCORDINGLY.

THE AUTHOR AND PUBLISHER DO NOT WARRANT THE PERFORMANCE, EFFECTIVENESS OR APPLICABILITY OF ANY SITES LISTED OR LINKED TO IN THIS BOOK. ALL LINKS ARE FOR INFORMATION PURPOSES ONLY AND ARE NOT WARRANTED FOR CONTENT, ACCURACY OR ANY OTHER IMPLIED OR EXPLICIT PURPOSE.

ANY TRADEMARKS, SERVICE MARKS, PRODUCT NAMES OR NAMED FEATURES ARE ASSUMED TO BE THE PROPERTY OF THEIR RESPECTIVE OWNERS, AND ARE USED ONLY FOR REFERENCE. THERE IS NO IMPLIED ENDORSEMENT IF WE USE ONE OF THESE TERMS.

NO PART OF THIS BOOK MAY BE REPRODUCED, STORED IN A RETRIEVAL SYSTEM, OR TRANSMITTED BY ANY OTHER MEANS: ELECTRONIC, MECHANICAL, PHOTOCOPYING, RECORDING, OR OTHERWISE, WITHOUT THE PRIOR WRITTEN PERMISSION OF THE AUTHOR.

ANY VIOLATION BY STEALING THIS BOOK OR DOWNLOADING OR SHARING IT ILLEGALLY WILL BE PROSECUTED BY LAWYERS TO THE FULLEST EXTENT. THIS PUBLICATION IS PROTECTED UNDER THE US COPYRIGHT ACT OF 1976 AND ALL OTHER APPLICABLE INTERNATIONAL, FEDERAL, STATE AND LOCAL LAWS AND ALL RIGHTS ARE RESERVED, INCLUDING RESALE RIGHTS: YOU ARE NOT ALLOWED TO GIVE OR SELL THIS GUIDE TO ANYONE ELSE.

THIS PUBLICATION IS DESIGNED TO PROVIDE ACCURATE AND AUTHORITATIVE INFORMATION WITH REGARD TO THE SUBJECT MATTER COVERED. IT IS SOLD WITH THE UNDERSTANDING THAT THE AUTHORS AND PUBLISHERS ARE NOT ENGAGED IN RENDERING LEGAL, FINANCIAL, OR OTHER PROFESSIONAL ADVICE. LAWS AND PRACTICES OFTEN VARY FROM STATE TO STATE AND IF LEGAL OR OTHER EXPERT ASSISTANCE IS REQUIRED, THE SERVICES OF A PROFESSIONAL SHOULD BE SOUGHT. THE AUTHORS AND PUBLISHER SPECIFICALLY DISCLAIM ANY LIABILITY THAT IS INCURRED FROM THE USE OR APPLICATION OF THE CONTENTS OF THIS BOOK.

COPYRIGHT BY HOWEXPERT™ (OWNED BY HOT METHODS)
ALL RIGHTS RESERVED WORLDWIDE.

Table of Contents

Recommended Resources..2
Introduction 6
Step 1: Do Your Hummingbird Homework 7
  Are Hummingbirds Found Where You Live? 7
Step 2: Sketch Your Blueprint......................................9
  Step 2.1 - Study Your Space 9
  Step 2.2 - Sketch Your Blueprint................................10
  Step 2.3 - Add Basic Elements 12
  Step 2.4 - Patios, Porches and Hanging Baskets..................14
Step 3: Hummingbird Feeders 16
  Step 3.1 - Why Use Feeders?.....................................16
  Step 3.2 - Choosing Your Hummingbird Feeder 17
  Step 3.3 - Sugar Water vs. Artificial Nectar 18
Step 4: Choosing Your Plants 21
  Step 4.1 - Perennials 21
    Bee Balm..22
    Columbine 22
    Cardinal Flower...23
    Coral Bells 23
    Strawberry Foxglove 23
    Red Hot Poker...24
    Great Blue Lobelia..24
    Beardtongue 25
    Bleeding Heart 25
  Step 4.2 - Annuals 25
    Petunias..26
    Impatiens...27
    Fuchsia...27
    Scarlet Sage 28
    Nasturtiums 29
    Snapdragon 29
  Step 4.3 - Vines 30
    Morning Glory...30
    Honeysuckle...31
    Trumpet Vine 32
  Step 4.4 - Shrubs and Trees 32
    Rose of Sharon 33
    Butterfly Bush 33
    Bottlebrush...34
    Crabapple Tree..34
    Eucalyptus Tree...35

English Hawthorn 36
Step 5: Plant Your Flowers 37
Step 5.1 - Soil Preparation 37
Step 5.2 - Planting 39
Step 5.3 - Maintenance 40
Step 6: Learn Your Species 42
Step 6.1 - Birdwatching Basics 42
Step 6.2 - Hummingbird Mini Field Guide 44
Ruby-throated Hummingbird 44
Black-chinned Hummingbird 44
Allen's Hummingbird 44
Broad-tailed Hummingbird 45
Calliope Hummingbird 45
Rufous Hummingbird 45
Lucifer Hummingbird 46
Anna's Hummingbird 46
Costa's Hummingbird 46
Step 7: Relax and Enjoy! 47
Step 7.1 - Hummingbird Gardening Fun Facts and Tips 47
Step 7.2 - Hummingbird Gardening with Native Wildflowers 48
About the Expert 51
Recommended Resources 52

Introduction

If you enjoy the sights and sounds of hummingbirds, you may be surprised to learn how easy and fun it is to create a garden for them within your space. Whether you have a large area to work with, or just a patio or porch, you can be a host for the hummingbirds in your local area by using these 7 simple steps to creating your own hummingbird garden.

Hummingbirds are a delightful addition to any garden since they bring iridescent beauty in flight and aerial dynamics at play. Hummingbirds also earn their keep by eating spiders, aphids, and gnats, among other pests. They are fast little zippers when they dive bomb each other at the feeder, yet peacefully graceful as they hum from flower to flower in the garden. A true miracle in flight, hummingbirds are capable of amazing aeronautics not found in other birds. Not only can they hover in midair, but they can also fly backward. Their wings beat so fast that it produces the humming sound we hear as they buzz by.

 Hummingbirds have good taste when it comes to plants. They enjoy red, tubular shaped blossoms, but will also visit other colors and shapes of blooms as well. Your garden can include a variety of plants, not just red ones. There is a large assortment of flowers, trees, and shrubs that attract hummingbirds, so it is usually very easy to find some of your favorites on the list.

Step 1: Do Your Hummingbird Homework

Are Hummingbirds Found Where You Live?

Hummingbirds are only found in the Western Hemisphere. Hummers are not physically able to cross the Atlantic Ocean, so they are not found naturally in Europe. North and Central America are the lands that they call home. In some areas, hummingbirds are only seen in migration. If you live in Canada, the United States, Mexico, Central America, the Leeward Islands, Hispaniola, or South America, then you can enjoy the rewarding hobby of hummingbird gardening.

As mentioned above, hummingbirds are not found all over the globe. A variety species are found in different countries and at different times of the year. Some areas are used as nesting grounds, and some areas only see hummingbirds during migration.

I find it easier to identify the hummers after they start coming to your garden than to learn which species I can expect to see beforehand, but you can choose to do it either way. There are several great websites for hummingbirds as well as a good old trip to the local library to check out books on this topic. I recommend obtaining a Hummingbird Field Guide which features images or drawings that you can take outside with you or keep handy on the windowsill closest to your garden. Then, when you see a hummingbird at one of your plants or feeders, you can quickly look it up using the pictures and then learn more about that species in the description section. There are many great online bird guides available, too. One of my favorites is the website for the Cornell Lab of Ornithology found at allaboutbirds.org Here you can identify birds not only by appearance but also by their songs and calls.

Hummingbirds are found in 48 different countries in the Americas, and many countries have several or more species. Only one species of hummingbird visits the eastern coast of the United States, the Ruby-throated Hummingbird. But the western half of the country is full of hummingbird varieties. Don't be discouraged if you live in the east because you can still enjoy gardening for hummers, even if it is only for one species. The Ruby-throated Hummingbird is the most widespread and popular of all hummers, and a gorgeous presence in your garden.

Step 2: Sketch Your Blueprint

Step 2.1 - Study Your Space

Whenever I am preparing to put in a new garden, the first thing I always begin with is studying the space I am going to be working with. Preferably, I like to watch the area over time and seasons to become familiar with the dynamics of light and shade that play out in the flower bed. The sun casts longer shadows in my yard during the winter time than it does during the summer time. So, I like to take this into consideration when planning for the garden because patches of ground that receive sunlight during the summer may be shady during winter. And vice versa in that areas that appear to be shady in the winter may get more sunshine during the summer.

Don't just think about the actual ground your garden will cover but also learn to think about the vertical spaces above ground as well. For example, try to project where the sun will be reaching about 3 feet above the soil level. This can help get your creative juices flowing when you imagine adding a trellis or lattice for your vines to cover with blooms.

I find it worthwhile to consider the logistics of the garden on the practical level, such as your water source and what else you may end up needing before you begin picking and planting your flowers. Measure how far your outdoor faucet is from the flower bed and be sure you have a long enough hose, for example. If you have a built-in sprinkler system, watch how and where the water reaches. You wouldn't want to plant right next to the sprinkler head because the force of the flow of water could damage your plant, and also because your plant might block the normal flow of water from the sprinkler, in which case the water would not reach its usual footage.

Another aspect I like to consider before digging is the way the shade in your space changes throughout the year. The amount of shade in winter is less because there aren't any leaves on the trees. Where the sun reaches the ground through the bare branches of winter will be shady when the trees grow their leaves again for the summer. Being familiar with the angles of sunlight at different times of the year in your planting area and planning ahead will help you to choose which plants will be best for your garden.

And, of course, you'll want to be able to see your hummingbird garden from your house ideally, so pick a location near a window if possible. I have arranged my living room so that my favorite chair is by the window where I can see about half of my front yard and the most popular hummingbird feeder. In a bigger yard, you can think about featuring a focal point to the garden, somewhat like a centerpiece on a table. It can be a patch of your favorite hummingbird flowers or even a hummingbird feeder.

Step 2.2 - Sketch Your Blueprint

After I have taken a little time to reflect on the space for the hummingbird garden, I find it is very helpful to draw a sketch of the way the space looks now, something like a quick blueprint. I use pencil because I often change my mind and need to erase something. Be sure to add any flower beds that already exist and any other unique items found in your yard. Include fences, sheds or outbuildings, and any plants, shrubs, trees, or lawn that is already there. You will want to incorporate these items into your new hummingbird garden. The wall of a shed provides a wonderful place to add lattice and transform the wall into a sea of blossoms for the hummers and for you to enjoy, too. Try to build from what you have to work with already. Many flowering vines attract hummingbirds and are easy to train to grow up a fence.

Next, draw your focal point, if you are creating one, in the sketch where you'll be able to see it easily. I know it is not always possible to have a perfect "bird's eye" view of everything in the garden from the house. Many of my flower beds are on the sides of the house I can't see from, or they are too low under the window to be seen. When I can't always watch from the comfort of my house, I do like to place a chair or garden bench outside where I can sit to view the activity in those unseen areas.

Now it's time for you to get creative and start thinking about what you are going to add to your yard. Start by thinking about where the plants are going to go before thinking about which plants to add. You can choose to add an entirely new flower bed or add to the ones you already have. An easy way to add to the garden instead of digging new garden beds is to use planters.

You can use planters for all kinds of handy things because they come in so many shapes and sizes. You can use wooden boxes and don't forget to add a window box wherever you can. These are one of my favorites because they truly do give you that "bird's eye" view since they're right in front of the window. Be sure when choosing or building your window box that it is deep enough and also sturdy enough. Gardens are very heavy, even when they are smaller! I've had my homemade window boxes come crashing down once I'd mounted them because they were not designed for the weight of the wet dirt after watering. The rectangular shaped window boxes that sit on a shelf are sometimes a little too shallow for anything but the daintiest of flowers.

Step 2.3 - Add Basic Elements

A hummingbird garden is most successful when it is actually a hummingbird habitat, and

this means adding more to it than just plants. The more basic elements you can add to your space then the more hummingbirds you will attract.

An uncommonly known fact about hummers is that they do not drink water like most birds do. Instead, they get all that they need from the nectar provided by your plants. However, they still need a water source for bathing. This doesn't need to be elaborate or expensive – it can be as simple as a shallow saucer of water. You can, of course, find lots of inspiration for a water source if you'd like. There are garden water misters available at garden stores, and fountains or even small waterfalls make an excellent place for the hummers to bathe and cool off.

Hummingbirds don't spend all of their time flying – they also need someplace to perch to rest. Trees and shrubs provide natural perches for hummers, so if you don't have any within 20 feet of your hummingbird garden, you may consider adding them. Butterfly Bush or Bee Balm is a beautiful addition that hummers love for their flowers and for perching. Crabapple trees draw in the hummers when they bloom in spring and keep them there as shelter for perching. If you can't add shrubs and trees to your garden, you can always make perches for the hummingbirds. This can be as easy as propping some dead branches around the edges of your garden, or you can even build your own. Remember how small a hummingbird's feet are when choosing your perches.

Trees and shrubs also give the hummingbirds a place to nest, which is my goal in my hummingbird garden. If they nest nearby, I know I'll get to see them often, so I work to cover all the basic needs of these tiny birds. I want to be able to observe the nest if possible, which I was able to do once before. I had made a flimsy planter out of an upside down straw hat with red petunias in it, and a mother hummingbird made her nest on it. I got so many hours of pleasure watching that little mama take care of her nestlings.

I hope to see another hummingbird nest in my garden someday, so I have chosen to add plants that provide nesting material, too. Hummers like to use fuzzy nesting materials such as pussy willows, eucalyptus trees, and lemon bottlebrush bushes. They also use the fuzz from dandelions and thistles, but few gardeners welcome these plants! Spider webs are another nesting material favorite of hummingbirds as well.

Trees can be both a sheltered perching place and sometimes also a food source for hummingbirds, too. They are known to feed on tree sap when they can find no other food. Moss and lichens are another nesting material favorite of the hummingbirds, and a tree often provides moss and lichens a place to grow.

Finally, most of the plants that attract hummingbirds prefer a mixture of sun and shade instead of full sun, so trees and shrubs can give shade to your space where the hummers can cool down while perching at rest. So, there are many good reasons to add trees and shrubs to your garden if you don't already have them.

As you make decisions about your hummingbird garden, add the new elements to your blueprint sketch. Slowly your garden will begin to take shape and become the garden you've visualized in your mind.

Step 2.4 - Patios, Porches and Hanging Baskets

Even if you are designing a small garden in a more limited space you can still benefit

from studying and sketching your plan beforehand. A quaint garden is a fabulous opportunity to think vertically because you really want to use precious space wisely. A lattice or trellis works great in this situation because they are found in all shapes and sizes which make it easier to find something to fit in your space. I find fabulous pieces of lattice at the local recycling center for pennies, or it is really easy to make your own framework for climbing vines.

If you don't have existing flower beds around your patio, you can use planters to add different levels to your garden by putting shorter ones in front and taller ones behind. You can still add many basic elements of the garden to your patio or porch just on a smaller scale.

I love making my own hanging baskets of all kinds. Just like planter pots, hanging baskets can be made out of all kinds of upside down containers if you can hang it. Or you can purchase lovely plant baskets and hangers of your own or buy the ready-made hanging plants at stores. I like to make my own because I can choose to make it entirely with plants for hummingbirds, whereas pre-planted store-bought baskets may only have one plant or have other plants in them that don't draw the hummers to them.

Another nice thing about hanging baskets is that they promote vertical planting as mentioned before. Baskets help to use the space above the ground, and if you hang several at different heights you will make smart use of your patio or porch. Remember to be sure you can easily reach hanging plants with a water wand or pitcher because they dry out so much faster than plants in the ground. You'll need to water frequently in hot weather.

Step 3: Hummingbird Feeders

Step 3.1 - Why Use Feeders?

You may wonder why you need a hummingbird feeder in your garden if you already have flowers for them, and the reason is that feeders sustain your hummers when flowers alone can't. Many hummingbird plants only flower for a short period of time, and many hummingbirds appear before or after the blooms, so having a feeder or two for the hummers can keep them coming when your blooms have passed. In addition, feeders by windows give excellent viewing opportunities. Some flowers come only once a year and only for a short period of time, yet others may bloom continuously throughout the season. In either case, it takes a little effort to keep plenty of flowers available at all times. Feeders are wonderful for filling the void.

One note I need to make about hummingbird feeders is that they are a commitment if you keep them up late into the season because your hummers will come to depend on them. I live in a semi-cold climate in the winter, and the hummers around here are not migrating but staying for the winter. They are almost completely dependent on feeders for their survival because there aren't any blooms or bugs to feed on in winter. When gardeners take down their feeders for the season, or even worse, keep them hanging there empty all winter, the hummers regard it as a winter food supply, and may not migrate in milder climates. Then when the feeder goes empty, the poor hummingbirds face death. So, the point I'm trying to make is that if you don't want to host the hummers year-round, you should bring your feeders in when the last blooms of summer fade so the birds won't get the wrong idea that the food will still be there.

Hummingbird feeders come in all shapes and sizes but usually have a few things in common, such as being the color red and having flower blooms around the feeding holes. You can purchase hummingbird feeders at most garden centers or birding stores, or you can make your own.

Step 3.2 - Choosing Your Hummingbird Feeder

Some hummingbird feeders are very elaborate while others are quite simple. There are a few things to keep in mind when making your choice of feeder before you buy. Make sure you pick a feeder with a clear reservoir so that you can easily see the level of liquid inside. I also like feeders that are easy to clean with a bottle brush and inexpensive to buy. Another feature I like in a hummingbird feeder is being leak-proof, but unless it's marked on the label you wouldn't be able to check for leaks before purchasing it.

Hummingbird feeders are usually a vertical style bottle, a horizontal style saucer, or basin shape, but I've seen some amazing creativity in homemade feeders, too. Most feeders are designed to hang, but I've placed hummingbird feeders on picnic tabletops and still attracted birds. I do think the hummers are much more vulnerable when feeding on a table, shelf, or ledge because predators can get to them easier.

The most important part of the hummingbird feeder is its color because hummers adore the color red. Almost every feeder will have some red on it somewhere to attract the birds to it, and if it doesn't then it should. Be sure to make your homemade feeders red, too. On the other hand, you'll want to try to avoid feeders with yellow because it attracts yellow jackets.

A nice feature on newer hummingbird feeders is feeding ports that are protected and/or ant moats for pest control. I really like this idea because it is not as messy as using vegetable oil on the wire or string that the feeder hangs on. With that technique, the ants would get stuck in the oil and never get to the food for the hummers, but the oil would soak down onto the top of the feeder making it very sticky and difficult to get clean. I've had quite a few issues with ants in my hummingbird feeders, as well as bees, and yellow jackets, especially toward the end of the season. So, I do like a feeder with pest control features.

Step 3.3 - Sugar Water vs. Artificial Nectar

Once you've obtained your hummingbird feeder you'll want to give your hummers the best food possible. I find there is some debate over which is better for the hummingbirds – homemade sugar water or the red, premade artificial nectar you can get at the store. I see many people buying it, but not too many folks have been as successful with it as they can be with sugar water. It's been my experience that the red nectar will attract the hummers to the feeder initially, but it doesn't keep them coming back because they just don't seem to like it once they've tasted it.

I highly recommend using sugar water you make yourself instead. It's more natural for the birds, and its super easy to make, just add one cup of sugar to four cups of water and simmer until the sugar is melted. Always be extra careful to let the sugar water cool completely before pouring it into your new hummingbird feeder because plastic feeders can melt if the water is still hot. Food coloring is not necessary and can be harmful to hummingbirds, so don't ever use it. The hummers will find your feeder from the red already on it. I like to make a double batch of sugar water and save the extra in a bottle or container in the refrigerator. Then, the next time you need to refill your feeder you will have it ready to use.

An active hummingbird feeder in the peak of the season needs to be cleaned and refilled with fresh sugar water approximately every five days or so because the sugar ferments in the feeder causing bacteria to grow that is harmful to the hummers. You can tell it's time to change your sugar water when the water appears cloudy. Never use honey for hummingbirds because it causes a fungus disease in the birds, and stay with the 1:4 ratio because sugar water that is too sweet can cause liver damage to the birds.

Now it is time to decide the best location for your feeder in your blueprint. For bigger gardens, I recommend using more than one feeder. Place your feeders where they can't be seen from each other because it can prevent one individual hummingbird from dominating all of the feeders. Hummingbirds are incredibly territorial and will fight over the feeder, so having more than one gives more hummingbirds a chance to eat.

Step 4: Choosing Your Plants

Now comes the fun part – choosing which plants to put in your hummingbird garden. As a general rule of thumb, hummingbirds are less attracted to white and yellow colors, so try not to use much of these in your flower choices. Also, hummingbirds do not have a strong sense of smell, so sweetly scented blooms are less attractive to them as well. Hummers feed by sight, and they are strongly attracted to the color red, so include as much of it as you would like.

Step 4.1 - Perennials

Plants that grow through spring and summer and then die in the fall and winter but return again in spring for more than 2 years are considered perennial. I think they're my favorites to work with because I just plant them once and they come back every year on their own. I make sure to water the roots of perennials throughout the autumn and winter to help them survive. In fact, I make it a point to water all of my gardens occasionally throughout the off season to keep roots alive. I water my planter pots even more frequently because it is easier for them to dry out faster even in the winter.

The perennials you can grow depends on your location, of course. Certain plants grow better in certain places, so you may have to do a little research to narrow it down to your specific country or region's best perennial choices. On the following pages, I've listed the perennials that hummingbirds love best in general and the ones I've had the most success with, including a short description with growing tips and the height of the plants. This is extremely useful information for planning where to place your plant choices in your garden blueprint. Remember to put taller plants behind shorter ones, etc. and draw them on your blueprint as you choose.

Bee Balm

Bee Balm is a garden favorite for hummingbirds and butterflies, too. It was a native wildflower until it was hybridized for gardens. It likes full sun and grows 2 to 4 feet tall, so be sure to place plants 18 – 24 inches apart. Although it is drought resistant, it does better with plenty of moisture in well-drained soil. Picking blooms encourages new flowers, and in the fall, it is important to cut Bee Balm down to a few inches tall. Be sure to mulch in spring.

Columbine

Columbines' delicate flowers come in a variety of colors and bloom during spring and early summer. They are not picky about the soil as long as it is well-drained. Columbine plants enjoy full sun, but not hot sun, so if summers are hot where you live you will want to plant them where there is shade in the afternoon. Space your plants about 1 – 2 feet apart. Columbine sometimes self-seeds and spreads out. Mulching will help keep the soil moist in summer and insulated in winter. You should keep them moist until they are established, and then water them once a week after that.

Cardinal Flower

The Cardinal Flower grows 3 – 4 feet tall and blooms from midsummer through early fall. It can tolerate poor drainage and doesn't require winter watering. Cardinal Flower grows well in part-shade but can handle full sun in cooler climates if kept moist. It blooms in red, white and pink, and should be placed 1 – 2 feet apart. Do not cut back in the fall.

Coral Bells

Coral Bells bloom from late spring to early summer in pink, white, coral and deep red. They prefer to grow in partial sun and in moist, well-drained soil. Coral Bells do great in planters. Their foliage can be bronze, red, silver, green or even purple, and since they are low-growing, they are perfect for the front borders of flower beds. They should be planted in the spring or the fall about 1 – 2 feet apart.

Strawberry Foxglove

Strawberry Foxglove blooms from spring through late summer in partial shade and grows 2 – 3 feet tall. This plant is very poisonous and should be handled with gloves on. Space plants 12 – 18 inches apart in rich soil. Strawberry Foxglove has blue-green or silver-gray foliage to accent the large tubular shaped blooms.

Red Hot Poker

The Red Hot Poker plant is native to South Africa and is an all-time favorite of the hummers. It grows 2 – 5 feet high and blooms from spring to fall in red, orange, coral, cream, and yellow colors. It is best to deadhead the spent flower spikes to promote more blooming. This plant loves an arid climate and does well in full sun. Plant 18 – 24 inches apart in loose, well-drained soil.

Great Blue Lobelia

This perennial plant is a blue relative of the Cardinal Flower that is in bloom from midsummer through fall. It stands 1 – 3 feet high and thrives in morning sun with afternoon shade. Great Blue Lobelia is not a drought-resistant plant, so you'll need to keep the soil moist. This plant is also poisonous if ingested.

Beardtongue

Beardtongue is a wildflower that is very successful in hot and sunny climates in dryer soil that is well drained. It is an ingredient in many Native American remedies. This plant blooms in spring and early summer and is 1 – 3 feet tall. Space your plants 12 – 18 inches apart in the spring. You should only fertilize Beardtongue once a year in the fall.

Bleeding Heart

The beautiful and dainty blooms of the Bleeding Heart plant are my favorite of all perennials, and the hummingbirds love them as well. Bleeding Heart grows best in shady areas of the garden and blooms in early spring with pink or white flowers. It needs to stay moist year-round even though it yellows and wilts after blooming and appears dead. It can be planted in spring or fall and needs only to be fertilized once a year in the spring when the new shoots appear. It stands 2 – 3 feet tall, and when the heart-shaped blooms come, their weight arches the stems.

Step 4.2 - Annuals

Annual plants only live for one growing season and need to be replaced every year, but this can be a good thing in a garden for a few reasons. Annuals generally bloom for the entire growing season and provide a constant food source when other plants have finished their blooming for that year. Annuals are quick and easy to add to your garden and can provide a splash of color. There are many varieties to pick from that attract hummingbirds, and they are usually relatively inexpensive. Another nice thing about annuals is that if you change your mind about where you put them, you don't have to dig them up to remove them. Just don't plant them there the next year. Annuals are also great for making your own hanging baskets and planter containers in spring.

On the following pages, you will find my recommendations of annual plants that will attract hummers and keep them returning to your garden all season.

Petunias

I grow petunias every single summer for the hummingbirds and for their light scent. They come in pink, purple, red, white, and yellow colors and can have variegated flowers which are two-toned. They like to sprawl out as they grow and will bloom for the whole growing season and into the fall. Plant them in full sun in well-drained soil after the last frost. The larger variety is best for pots and hanging baskets and the smaller variety thrives growing in the ground.

**Impatiens**

I like to use Impatiens in my wheelbarrow planter every season. It's not the deepest planter, but this little annual does quite well there. This is the perfect plant for the shadowy corners of your yard because it loves shade to part sun. It blooms in orange, pink, purple, red, white, and yellow from midsummer to fall. Impatiens can grow anywhere from 6 – 30 inches tall. For lower plants, place 8 – 12 inches apart when planting in moist soil. The closer these plants are then the taller they will grow. Be sure to keep them moist by watering regularly.

**Fuchsia**

Fuchsias are very popular with hummingbirds and are usually grown in hanging baskets or planter containers. They can grow into a large bush when planted in the ground. Fuchsias come in a grand array of colors and shapes with delicate, fancy flowers. The different varieties were bred for different needs with some tolerating certain climates better than others.

In general, fuchsias prefer cooler temperatures between 55 - 80° F to continue producing blooms. In regions where summer temperatures soar they should be kept in the shade. Fuchsias are picky about the soil, it can't be too wet, too dry, or too hot. When planting them in pots or baskets use a potting soil because it has the best mix for the plants, it will be more lightweight, and will drain better. Otherwise, be sure to add compost to the soil your fuchsias will be growing in. In either case, always be sure to keep your fuchsia moist and never let it dry out, especially in containers.

Fuchsias require fertilizer for best results. You can over-winter your fuchsia baskets and planters by bringing them indoors before the first hard freeze and placing them in a cool location where the temperature is between 45 - 60° F. Cut them back halfway and water occasionally, to keep them from drying out. The leaves will drop leaving bare stems. Bring them back outdoors in spring after all danger of frost has passed and thoroughly water. When new growth appears, you can trim the branches and pinch the tips until flower buds appear for bushier plants.

__Scarlet Sage__

Scarlet Sage was originally from Brazil and is also known as Blood Sage, Indian Fire, and Scarlet Salvia because of the vividly deep red color of the flowers. This plant stays in bloom from early spring through fall and grows 2 – 4 feet tall. Blooms can also be pink or white. Scarlet Sage can grow well in rocky, sandier soil with good drainage. It prefers full sun but will grow in partial shade and is great for borders and rock gardens. Deadhead spent flower spikes to encourage more blooms and for bushier plants.

Nasturtiums

Nasturtiums are fun and easy to grow. I like to plant them in my front flower bed after the spring bulbs have bloomed. They quickly fill the entire bed and bloom from late spring through fall. I sow seeds directly into the ground about half an inch deep and 10 – 12 inches apart, and they appear in 7 – 10 days. Nasturtiums are great because they do so well in poor soil. In fact, fertilizer is not recommended for these plants because it causes them to bloom less. Nasturtiums are available in smaller bushy varieties and larger vine-like varieties. Plant them in soil that is well-drained and in full sun because they will not bloom as much in the shade. These plants are completely edible, and their flower meaning is patriotism.

Snapdragon

Snapdragons are available in gorgeous color combinations and in different sizes which makes them very versatile. Snapdragons can be dwarf-sized, intermediate or tall stems ranging from 3 inches to 6 feet. They prefer the cooler weather of early spring and fall, and may not bloom as well in summer's heat. They are able to stand frost, so they can be put out into the garden in late winter so that they can bloom before the weather turns hot. Snapdragons come in every color except blue.

Although they hate the heat, they love full sun and should be planted in well-drained soil. You can manipulate them to be bushier and bloom better by clipping the top stem and side shoots, and then in early summer when the blooms start fading you should clip them back about one-half to one-third for more blooms in the fall. Tall varieties may need to be staked to stand upright.

Step 4.3 - Vines

Growing vines for the hummers is creative and fun because you get to add decorative trellises, lattice, arbors, arches, and framework or fencing for the vines to grow on and the hummingbirds love it. I like to work with vines to train them to grow in creative ways. As you make decisions about the right plants for your hummingbirds be sure to use vines for vertical coverage and add them into your blueprint. My favorites are on the following pages.

Morning Glory

Morning Glory is an annual climbing vine with trumpet-shaped flowers and heart-shaped leaves that bloom in summer and lasts until fall. They can grow as much as 15 feet in just one growing season, so you'll want something for them to grow on with lots of space. They quickly twist around mailbox stands, fencing gates, and whatever else you can provide for them. They bloom in pink, purple-blue, magenta, or white, and are grown from seeds that are highly toxic if ingested. Plant them as soon as the ground temperature reaches 64° F by first filing the seeds only long enough to break the skin, and then soak them for 24 hours. Sow the seeds about ¼ inch deep and 6 inches apart. Choose a very sunny location that provides shelter from the wind.

<u>Honeysuckle</u>

Honeysuckle is a popular and vigorous vine to grow that attracts hummingbirds and butterflies, and it even produces a fruit in the fall that songbirds love to treat on. A longtime favorite fragrance from their intricate blooms permeates the air around them. Honeysuckle is very vigorous and tolerant of the heat. It blooms very heavily in the spring and then sporadically during summer.

Most often it is supported by a structure like fences, arbors, trellis and latticework, but it can also be grown as a ground cover or in a container. Honeysuckle loves the full sun for the best results, but it will tolerate some shade. They need to be fertilized in the spring and again in mid-season and require moderate watering after that.

Be sure to secure the support structure before planting, and then place the plants 2 – 3 feet apart from each other and 6 – 12 inches from their support structure. As it grows, tie the vines to the support using a stretchy material, such as nylons, so it won't cut into the vines. Once well-established, you can prune the vines back in winter for better blooming.

Trumpet Vine

Trumpet Vine is famous for attracting hummingbirds and a staple plant for a hummingbird garden. However, it can grow as much as 30 – 40 feet in just one season, so space is something to prepare for when growing Trumpet Vine. It is also known as Trumpet Creeper because of the way the roots spread underground. In fact, it should not be grown by buildings as the roots can actually do damage. If planted in full sun, Trumpet Vine will produce yellow- -orange and red tubular shaped flowers all summer and into the fall, although it blooms less in shady areas.

A vigorous and hardy plant, Trumpet Vine is tolerant of almost any soil type. It is very difficult to get rid of once planted, so choose a location you can live with over time. Trumpet Vine requires a sturdy support structure in place prior to planting. Pruning is usually needed to keep it under control and is the only maintenance it needs except for watering when needed. Pruning is best done in the spring. Do not fertilize Trumpet Vine.

Step 4.4 - Shrubs and Trees

If you have a large space for your hummingbird garden you may even be able to add shrubs and trees. These are not only great for the flowers they have but also for the perches, shade, and shelter they provide. Trees and shrubs are a more permanent addition, so plan their location carefully and allow plenty of room to grow. Don't forget to draw them into your blueprint as well.

Rose of Sharon

A Rose of Sharon bush seems to always be buzzing with hummingbirds and is an elegant choice for any garden. Originally from eastern Asia, this bush practically grows itself and needs little maintenance. Available in white, red, pink, and purple, Rose of Sharon will bloom throughout the summer. It can grow to stand 9 – 12 feet tall and spread out to 10 feet wide, and it often reseeds itself making new bushes. Rose of Sharon needs rich and slightly acidic soil that is well drained for best results, but it can grow in almost any dirt that is not soggy or bone-dry. It is best to prune your Rose of Sharon in early spring before buds form or in late fall after the leaves have dropped off. The flowers form on the current year's growth.

Butterfly Bush

Butterfly Bush blooms from summer through fall with purple, pink, red, white, or yellow flowers that can be up to 12 inches long and permeate the air with sweet fragrance. It can grow up to 6 – 8 feet high in almost any soil type. Plant Butterfly Bush in the full sun in the spring or fall about 5 – 10 feet apart. In Northern climates, this bush may die down to the roots during winter and then be late to return in spring. Even if the stems survive the winter, it is best to prune them back severely to encourage blooms on the new growth. Do not fertilize Butterfly Bush, and only water generously when in growth and sparingly after that.

Bottlebrush

Bottlebrush varieties can grow from a bush into a tree over time and draw hummingbirds like a magnet. Most bottlebrush blooms in summer with fuzzy flowers in shades of red and crimson with one variety that produces yellow blooms. Bottlebrush prefers more mild climates and should be grown in pots that can be brought inside in places with harsh winters. Grow in a sunny location in well-drained soil for best results. Hold back on pruning if you want a bush, or prune it to one trunk to grow it into a tree.

Crabapple Tree

Crabapple trees are available in a large assortment of varieties, shapes, colors, and sizes to pick from all with gorgeous blossoms in the spring and fruit in the fall. Crabapple trees are pretty tough and can adapt to hard winters or poor soil. They usually have blossoms in April and May that are red to pink to white, and their foliage has inviting colors in the fall. Some varieties of crabapples are edible and others are just ornamental.

They are drought-resistant but should not be planted in low-lying areas that might get soggy in winter and spring. They thrive in the full sun. They are very hardy and do even better when planted in rich, slightly acidic soil with good drainage. If you choose a bare-root crabapple tree, it will need to be planted in the spring. Container-grown or the burlap-style root balls can be planted as soon as the soil is workable or any other time during the season. Fertilizing and pruning are very minimal.

Eucalyptus Tree

Native to Australia, the Eucalyptus tree cannot tolerate temperatures below 50° F. If you live in a colder climate, you can still grow Eucalyptus in a large container that you can move for winter shelter. Keep in mind, these trees can get as much as 30-180 feet tall in perfect growing conditions, so leave room to grow if you plant in the ground.

Eucalyptus needs to be in the full sun in well-drained soil. Water before and after planting, and try not to spread out the roots because they do not like being disturbed. It can be planted in spring or in fall, and once established, it requires minimal watering, except if in a pot. Eucalyptus does not require fertilizer, but it is best to prune them to keep them under control. It sheds its bark as well as its leaves in fall, so prepare to clean up a little mess because the bark is very flammable. The flowers are unique because they do not have petals, just stamens, and they bloom in creamy white, yellow, pink and red.

English Hawthorn

The English Hawthorn tree is very popular with the hummers when it blooms in spring and it produces berries in fall, which are very popular with people for medicinal reasons. It likes full sun in slightly acidic soil. The English Hawthorn tree can grow up to 25 feet high with lavender, pink, red, and white flowers. I always thought they looked like little roses, and, like roses, this tree does have thorns to beware of. Turf will not grow underneath an English Hawthorn tree.

Step 5: Plant Your Flowers

Step 5.1 - Soil Preparation

It's time to break new ground and start preparing the soil for your plants. In my first gardens, I used a shovel and turned the soil by hand, which I do not recommend unless it is a small garden area to be worked. For medium to large garden plots, I use a small rototiller to break new ground. You'll have to wait until the ground thaws and the soil isn't too wet.

I usually remove any lawn or weeds that are already growing there and dispose of them in the compost pile. Do not rototill the lawn and weeds right into the soil because they will only cause more grass and weeds to come back. I think this stage is the hardest part of putting in a new garden because it can be a little back-breaking.

Once the lawn has been removed, you can begin to till the soil. There are many additives you can put into your soil for your plants, and it sometimes depends on what you are trying to grow. Most plant stores sell a soil-testing kit that you can use to see what kind of soil you have in your space. Often, you can send your soil samples to your local Cooperative Extension office for testing. You then know what kinds of additives to use.

Most soil is clay, sandy, or loam, and you'll need to add nutrients, organic matter, and/or inorganic matter for best results. Some organic soil additives commonly used are compost, manure, sphagnum peat moss, and topsoil. Inorganic additives include sulfur, lime, perlite, gypsum, and vermiculite. For container gardening, it is very important to use potting soil. This dirt is specially blended for planter pots with organic and inorganic matter and additional elements for moisture retention, fertilizer, pest control and aeration. Many pre-mixed soils are available for specific plants, too, such as Orchid mix and African Violet soil.

I've tried many things in my yard, and one thing I've learned is that if you can keep it simple you won't get overwhelmed. I've learned not to "feed the weeds" so to say by not using all of these additives all at once and all over the garden bed. There's going to be space left between your plants, especially in the beginning before they get growing. And in that space, there is high weed potential, too. I tend to add the soil amendments to the planting zone and not to the entire zone. All those lovely nutrients and organic matter will fertilize the weeds just as well as your plants, so I don't use the additives in between my plants. I make a wheel barrel full of garden dirt with the additives mixed into it, and I use that to fill the immediate area of the plants and about a one-foot radius around the plant for it to grow into. I find it much easier to mix a wheel barrel full of planting soil than to mix bags of expensive additives into the entire garden plot. Then I can wheel the mixed dirt around to the different planting sites and get the flowers in the ground.

Step 5.2 - Planting

Often, not all of your plants will get planted at the same time. Some may be starts in little pots while others may be sown from seeds. Hardy plants can go out earlier than their warm weather-loving friends. Planting day if always so exciting! At this point, you finally get to start seeing your hummingbird garden come together, but there's still some work to do now.

Place your plant starts where they are supposed to go according to your blueprint. When space provides, try to plant 3 or more of the same plant for more nectar. Then follow the planting directions that usually accompany the starts on a little tab in their dirt or on the box or bag your plant start came in. If you are planting something that was featured in the previous step, then you can use the directions provided in the plant description there. Each plant has its own criteria for planting and growing, so if you do not find instructions you can always go online for the best tips for that particular plant.

If you have a lot of starts to plant, don't work too hard to get it all done in a day. Keep your starts moist in their little pots while they are waiting for you to get to them. After your plants are in the ground be sure to very gently water them well. This helps to remove air pockets and get the plant settled in and going.

I live in an area that is very wet most of the year, and I know I have snails and slugs to worry about. I have seen a whole cucumber leveled overnight by snails and slugs, so I always try to be proactive about pests. Some gardeners use chemicals and some do not. It is up to you. Keep in mind that some pesticides are harmful to the hummers as well as the pests.

There are many organic ways to battle snails and slugs, or you can just use snail bait. As long as the hummers don't come into contact with it, things should be fine. At any rate, be sure to think about what kind of protection your tender new plants will need now that they are outside.

Step 5.3 - Maintenance

After many years of hummingbird gardening, I find myself leaning towards the low maintenance flowers, shrubs, and trees because I am not as young as I used to be and because I have so many other projects in the garden going all the time. I find that the low maintenance plants are a wonderful time saver for busy people. By low maintenance, I mean minimal fertilizing, pruning, training, and my least favorite, weeding. I like to put straw or other ground cover between my plants to minimize weeds and help to keep moisture in longer.

The plants featured in the previous step have a description of what kind of care to expect to have to do to maintain them at their best after planting. For some, you'll need to deadhead the spent blooms or prune in the fall, and for others, you will only have to fertilize once a year or so. But for all of the plants you put in your garden, you will have to weed.

Weeding is my most dreaded task in the garden, but it has become much easier with the right tools and ground cover. Shop around for the tools that will best help you stay ahead of weeds in your situation. I don't like to be on my knees or bending over for long periods of time, so I really appreciate long handled tools that enable me to stand for most of the time. In my largest garden, there was enough space between the plants to rototill with a cultivator, which was nice and made the garden look so neat and tidy.

Step 6: Learn Your Species

Depending on where you live, you may see many species or just the Ruby-throated hummingbird. If your area enjoys more than one species, then you can learn to differentiate as well as identify species in your garden and even identify individual birds. Quite often, the same individuals will visit your garden all season, and then the same individuals will come back to your garden again the next year.

To me, this is the part that makes all of the work worth it, watching and identifying the hummers in my yard busy finding nectar and guarding their turf. Over time, you almost get to know them more personally if you've learned how to identify your individual hummers.

Step 6.1 - Birdwatching Basics

The first step is to learn a little bit about hummingbirds in your local area so you'll know what they like. Knowing a little bit about the hummingbirds makes it easier to take good care of them when they come to your garden. Check out your local Audubon Society, birding stores, and even birding clubs to learn about which species you may hope to attract in your region.

The next step is to get a Field Guide, and I recommend getting binoculars, too. You will need both for identifying your species. I have included a mini field guide in the next pages for your convenience and to help you get started.

There are certain things you learn to look for on the hummers that give you clues to their species. Here are some of the features you will look for when you spot a hummingbird in your garden. The males are the ones with the flashy, iridescent throats, and the females are not as showy, so they are much harder to identify.

The beautiful jeweled throat of a male hummingbird is called a gorget. The females won't have one. There are some species that have a brighter-colored region on their crowns and foreheads which is known as a helmet.

As you spot the hummingbirds in your flowers, take note of the bird's colors and where they are located on the bird. Take a close look at the hummingbird's tail and try to see if it has white or reddish-brown spots and where they are on the tail. Pay attention to the beak, too, as some are longer than others and one species even sports a red beak!

Make a mental note of the hummingbird's shape, size, and its behaviors. Better yet, you can try to take a photo of the hummer that you can reference later. If photography isn't quite your forte, you can keep a pen and notebook handy to jot down the bird's features while you are watching it. I then grab my field guide and look up the hummingbird's species. Some birdwatchers keep a journal of all the birds they have spotted in the wild.

Step 6.2 - Hummingbird Mini Field Guide

Ruby-throated Hummingbird

In the Ruby-throated Hummingbird, both males and females are a metallic green color on their backs (above) and are a grayish color on their bellies (underneath). Their size is about 3 to 3 3/4 ", and they spread their wings to about 4 to 4 ¾". The male's throat looks black until it flashes red or orange in sunlight, and the female's throat has white spots. Males also have a tail that is somewhat forked.

Black-chinned Hummingbird

Black-chinned Hummingbirds are also metallic green above and grayish white underneath. Males have a black chin with an iridescent purple stripe at the base. The female's 3 broad tail feathers sport white tips. The bill is black.

Allen's Hummingbird

Male Allen's hummers have an iridescent red throat with the top and back of its head a metallic bronze green. The chest is white with a white spot behind the eye. The sides of its face and chest are cinnamon rufous colored. The male's orange tail feathers are pointed. The females also have metallic green above and white on their chin, chest, and throat.

Broad-tailed Hummingbird

The Broad-tailed Hummingbird is slightly larger and has a much broader tail than other hummingbirds. Males wear a gorgeous rosy red gorget with green above and on its crown and white underneath. Females are larger than males with a pale eye ring.

Calliope Hummingbird

The tiny Calliope Hummingbird is the smallest bird in the United States. The beautiful male has a brilliant magenta and white throat while the female has a cinnamon buff chest and belly with a whitish throat. Both sexes have green above.

Rufous Hummingbird

The male Rufous Hummingbird is known for his fiery orange back and belly and his iridescent throat and the females are green above and on the tail with a spot of orange on their throat and buff patches. Their reputation precedes them as the most rambunctious hummingbird.

Lucifer Hummingbird

The Lucifer Hummingbird male boasts an iridescent purple gorget and a curved beak with a forked tail. The females have green backs with buff underneath. Lucifer hummers are easily chased off by other hummingbirds due to their lower rank.

Anna's Hummingbird

The male Anna's Hummingbird has a pinky reddish head and gorget with gray and green on their bodies. They have a shorter beak and a broader tail, and they are stockier than other hummers.

Costa's Hummingbird

A male Costa's Hummingbird has an iridescent violet crown and gorget that extends with green above. Females are white underneath and sometimes have violet feathers on their white throats.

Step 7: Relax and Enjoy!

Now is the time to reap the benefits of all your hard work by taking a much deserved break in your hummingbird garden. Remember to give the hummingbirds a chance to find your flowers and feeders. Sometimes they appear almost instantly and other times it may take longer. Young starts may not have many blooms in the beginning of the season to draw the hummers in, so be sure to keep your feeders replenished with fresh sugar water.

It is not uncommon for the hummingbird activity to taper off during summer because the hummers are nesting and caring for the young, and also because there are so many other food sources available by summer, such as insects. Don't let this discourage you, keep refilling your feeders and taking care of your plants. The hummingbirds will return.

Step 7 .1 - Hummingbird Gardening Fun Facts and Tips

- All hummingbirds have the fastest metabolisms of any animal, even 100x faster than the largest land animal, the elephant.
- A hummingbird's heart beats 1260x per minute, and its breathing rate is 250 breaths per minute!
- A hummingbird's wings beat 70x per second generally, and 200x per second when diving. To keep up this fast pace, hummingbirds need

to eat ½ their body weight daily, feeding every 15 – 20 minutes or up to 8x per hour.
- Hummingbirds can burn up to 12,000 calories per day. This is why it is so important for hummers to have plenty of food sources in your garden.
- Hummingbirds are the smallest of all the bird family, and the Bee Hummingbird is the smallest of all the hummingbirds, weighing in at less than 2.5 grams and measuring only 5 cm.
- The average-sized hummingbird is approximately 3-5 inches tall. This is good to know so you can try to leave lots of space between your plants for their wings.
- An easy way to determine if your planter pots need to be watered is to simply lift them; they will be heavy if they're still wet and light if they are dry.

Step 7.2 - Hummingbird Gardening with Native Wildflowers

In my earlier hummingbird gardens, I always used plants that were either perennials, annuals or a hybrid mix. But I've since learned that hummingbirds actually prefer native wildflowers over the others because native plants produce a higher quality of nectar for them. Wanting what's best for the birds and the garden, too, I began a new interest in native wildflower gardening. I am still developing my skills in this area, but I want to share what I do know because I think it's an important piece of hummingbird gardening.

What I used to think were weeds and diligently kept out of my hummingbird gardens turned out to be native plants that were good for the garden and the hummers, too. I was fascinated with this whole new angle to hummingbird gardening but didn't know where to start. So, I began Googling and found some really great resources for getting started, such as the local chapter of the Native Plant Society and the local Cooperative Extension office.

Luckily, there is an arboretum in my locale that holds a sale only once a year where I can go, to buy individual native plants, but the sale was a couple of months away. So, I also turned to plant guides for the wildflowers in my region so I would have an idea of what I was looking for. I then examined my gardens and yard for any plants that might already be native and I just didn't know it. I checked out some books on the subject from the library as well, and soon I was recognizing native plants all around me. I'd spot them growing on the side of the road or in empty vacant lots

There is much to be said about the native flowers in your local region if you take the time to notice them. They are specially adapted to the local climate and conditions, and since they are so hearty they actually require less maintenance. Many native plants are drought-resistant and require less water. They all have a sweet beauty to bring to your hummingbird garden, too. And the biggest selling point for me is that the hummingbirds like them better than the hybrids and annuals I was used to gardening with. So,

I recommend learning how to add native wildflowers to your hummingbird garden to help restore a small piece of natural habitat for the hummers.

About the Expert

Essie Thorn has been gardening for hummingbirds for 35 years in the Pacific Northwest, and what started as a hobby has become her real area of expertise, mostly from years of trial and error, and from keeping good notes about what worked and what didn't.

As an avid collector of all things hummingbird, Essie has been hooked on birds and blooms since childhood and has designed many hummingbird gardens over the years.

In addition to this guide, Essie has been published in Rocks & Gems magazine and writes articles for several blogs. You can email Essie at essiethorn@yahoo.com, and check out her website/blog at essiethorn.wordpress.com.

HowExpert publishes quick 'how to' guides on all topics from A to Z by everyday experts. Visit HowExpert.com to learn more.

Recommended Resources

- HowExpert.com – Quick 'How To' Guides on All Topics from A to Z by Everyday Experts.
- HowExpert.com/free – Free HowExpert Email Newsletter.
- HowExpert.com/books – HowExpert Books
- HowExpert.com/courses – HowExpert Courses
- HowExpert.com/membership – HowExpert Membership Site
- HowExpert.com/writers – Write About Your #1 Passion/Knowledge/Expertise & Become a HowExpert Author.
- HowExpert.com/resources – Additional HowExpert Recommended Resources
- YouTube.com/HowExpert – Subscribe to HowExpert YouTube.
- Instagram.com/HowExpert – Follow HowExpert on Instagram.
- Facebook.com/HowExpert – Follow HowExpert on Facebook.

Made in the USA
Monee, IL
06 July 2020